MARRIAGE MINISTRY
Working Together with Family

Carol Linda Brown

Copyright © 2018 by Carol Linda Brown

All rights reserved. No part of this book may be used or reproduced by any means, graphic, electronic, or mechanical, including photocopying, recording, taping or by any information storage retrieval system without the written permission of the publisher except in the case of brief quotations embodied in critical articles and reviews.

Carol Linda Brown/Rejoice Essential Publishing
PO BOX 512
Effingham, SC 29541
www.republishing.org

Scripture quotations marked (NLT) are taken from the Holy Bible, New Living Translation, copyright ©1996, 2004, 2015 by Tyndale House Foundation. Used by permission of Tyndale House Publishers, Inc., Carol Stream, Illinois 60188. All rights reserved.

Scriptures marked NKJV are taken from the NEW KING JAMES VERSION (NKJV): Copyright© 1982 by Thomas Nelson, Inc. Used by permission. All rights reserved.

Copyright © 2018 Carol Linda Brown

Author's website: www.buildthemontherock.org

Unless otherwise indicated, Scripture is taken from the King James Version and the American Standard Version (ASV).

All rights reserved.

Marriage Ministry Working Together With Family/ Carol Linda Brown

ISBN-10: 1-946756-30-X
ISBN-13: 978-1-946756-30-5
Library of Congress Control Number: 2018951269

CONTENTS

ACKNOWLEDGEMENTS..................1

PREFACE.........................2

INTRODUCTION...................4

LESSON 1:   Standing Together.....................6

LESSON 2:   Respect For Each Other...........10

LESSON 3:   Communication.......................13

LESSON 4:   Which Comes First
            Marriage or Ministry?.............18

LESSON 5:   Healthy Marriage....................22

LESSON 6:   Prayer: Pray Tighter................26

LESSON 7:   Sexual Intimacy......................29

LESSON 8:   The Vows..............................35

LESSON 9:   Unequally Yoked...................38

LESSON 10:   Understanding How to
                      Choose Your Mate.................41

CONCLUSION..47

ABOUT THE AUTHOR................................49

REFERENCES..51

When I say I love you, please believe it's true.
When I ... love you.
When ... goodbye, remember me ... don't cry.
Because ... the day I die.
A million tears up ... shines brighter I can't
... I love ... returns a love ...
a love that comes from me to you...

ACKNOWLEDGEMENT

I am humbled by the tremendous support from my husband Victor. He always pushes and encourages me to pursue my dreams. Victor, I will always love you. I thank Kat in a special way for helping me with my book. I also thank Kimberly Moses for spiritually connecting with me and completing my book for me. Thanks to my wonderful mother who gave me a prophecy that I would do this someday. Special thanks to all those who prayed and supported me in this ministry. I am so grateful to God for planting and birthing this gift inside of my heart to help others to be restored in their family and marriages; I trust and believe many will be healed and delivered. I truly thank you, Lord.

PREFACE

But God hath chosen the foolish things of the world to confound the wise; and God hath chosen the weak things of the world to confound the things which are mighty; - 1 Corinthians 1:27 KJV

I decided to write this book because I love to encourage people, particularly believers, to live a full life and encourage them to walk as they are called. Yes, everything is possible within the will of God, including your marriage to be a successful one! God intended for us to walk together as one in loving Holy Matrimony, letting no man put us under. I see it is God's will that we be one with each other. I pray and believe this book will change the hearts and minds of marriages all around the world.

This book is written for Christians by a committed Christian. I make no apology for that. I can only testify truthfully to what I have personally lived. If you do not believe in the Lord Jesus Christ as your Lord, Savior, and King, You will struggle with the words in this book. I do not pertain to have all the answers, but I know a man who does! His name is Jesus. The advice I give in this book, if followed, will put God in the center of your marriage. And the rest is the experiences that worked for my husband and

I. If you're not a believer you will receive some practical encouraging habits from this book. For a full abundant life, getting Jesus in the center of your life is truly the only way.

INTRODUCTION

There are so many marriages and families under attack by the fiery darts of this world—divorces, broken families, children straying away, even in Christian homes. It appears that there needs to be some strong ministering with some spiritual warfare to restore our marriages and families.

1. Mission

We see this training as a restorative tool to repair and return families back to their first love, the Lord Jesus Christ. It is time for us to stop the lies of the devil in this world in regards to marriages and families. It is time for us to expand the Kingdom of God in our homes and in our marriages, to bring marriages and families back to the original order that God intended from the beginning!

2. Sessions

- Standing Together
- Respect for Each Other
- Communication
- Marriage Comes First
- Healthy Marriage
- Prayer: Pray Tighter

- Sexual Intimacy
- No Dominating
- Vows
- Unequally Yoked
- Understanding How To Choose Your Mate

3. Training: A Restorative Tool

- We are training from an in-depth standard, not as the marriage in the old but of today – a fresh and a new revelation.
- We will open up revelation to the learner by looking up scriptures, the natural, Hebrew and Greek words.
- What you will get in the training will restore your marriage, prepare you for marriage, and prepare your family as a whole
- We also will take this tool further than a class by continuing with counseling and offering sessions in your homes.
- We will not teach surface level marriage classes, but full-impact classes in order to heal one marriage and multiply more and more marriages. So, you as couples will be able to take dominion over your own marriages and families.
- We will do movie clips, some games ~ comparable to the Newly Wed game and more.

- We will have other tools such as, tapes and books as on-going personal counseling after the class is over. This is for home use and also for couples that may have mates that may not want to attend for some reasons.

4. Session Standards

- You are not to miss more than three days, or you will be obligated to retake the entire class to receive a certificate.
- In each session, the facilitators will present the lesson and assign take-home quizzes which will be homework for individual couples who will work together as a team to share with the class at the following session.
- Complete all assignments and turn them in before the course ends.
- There will be certificates for each person upon completion of the class.
- .At the final session, there will be a drawing for a couple to accompany the Browns on an evening date.

LESSON 1

STANDING TOGETHER

United We Stand, Divided We Fall

(Philippians 4:1-5)

The above scriptures are examples of working together. Serving in ministry or not in ministry is possible, but can be done usually with communication and cooperation which brings the essential ingredients. You must be on the same page, reading from the same playbook, if you will. I remember just the opposite happening once and only once in our ministry and lots of times with our children. One time, my son asked if he could go and stay with a friend overnight, I told him, yes, and my husband told him no, that was the last time that happened. We make sure we function as a unified-front by communicating with one another. We discuss things prior to our services to ensure that there are no surprises!

Serving together will undoubtedly require understanding one another's strengths and weaknesses. There is no room for intimidation or feeling jealous because of what works in the other. The Word of God says that I leave my father and mother to cleave to my wife (Genesis 2:24). This says to us that we are now one with each other and not one with mom and dad any longer. We should work out our differences with prayer, fasting, communication and also the Word of God.

Respectfully Leaving Your Father and Mother

The Bible tells us that we are to leave our father and mother and to cleave to each other after we marry. It tells us, "Therefore a man shall leave his father and mother and be joined (cleave) to his wife, and they shall become one flesh" (Genesis 2:24).

The best times are those when together we truly seek to serve and follow the Lord and His plans for our lives; that's a promise, a promise is a promise. But there are a few other things I have learned as well because it hasn't been smooth sailing all the way. Like any married couple, we have had our share of ups and downs, good times and not so good times, and some downright bad times.

Years ago, we threatened each other over the phone that we were going to breakup, but with the help of the Lord, we came together. There was another time, we were in Battle Creek going out to eat and we had a big argument. The Lord told us to pull over into a parking lot, to just sit and be quiet, so we did. We sat for about 20 minutes or more. We looked at each other and said, "Are you ready to go eat now?" We said, "Yes." The good part about it was when we got to the restaurant, there was a couple that came in whom we were in ministry with some years ago. We had not seen one another in a long time, and we got to fellowshipping and found that they had a call on them for marriage ministry, as well. So the devil meant it for our bad, but God meant it for our good.

LESSON 2

RESPECT FOR EACH OTHER

Where Two Lives Are Joined As One By God

(Exodus 3:5; Matthew 19:6)

There should always be unity between you and your spouse. When there is a need for correction, it should not be done behind the pulpit or in front of others. That is surely not the way to lead by example. Couples should never give signs to others that there is trouble in their marriage. There is room and a grace for both to serve if respect and communication are the building blocks on which your marriage and ministry are built upon. Serving together in ministry will certainly require prayer and seeking out the Holy Spirit's wisdom for your particular situation.

We do not want to open the door of disrespect to our spouses. When this occurs, someone will be ready to make a move onto your spouse. They or someone who is interested in your spouse will wait for signs; any sign that says there is trouble in the camp. Never criticize your spouse in public, or run them down, or humiliate them in any way.

I once said something like, "A wife should be her husband's biggest fan." (It's the other way around, too). Build your spouse up to others. Praise and admonish him/ her and his/ her achievements to others. Whatever you are thinking about saying (negatively), save it for home to voice aloud; by then, it will probably be less important anyway and your moments of praising will affect your own attitude too.

A spouse can do what no one else can do. Pray for your partner at the deepest level because you both know one another so well. You both know how to pray for each other better than anyone else does. And if the snoring wakes you at night, take that as a moment to lay hands on him/ her and pray; it might just be a God-given opportunity. Press to show a good example in front of your children because you are the first example or role model they will see.

When your children see you with no respect for each other, most of the times, they will not have any respect for others and could also have problems building relationships with others or their mate-to-be.

LESSON 3

COMMUNICATION

Victor's viewpoint

(1 Peter 4:11; Ephesians 4:29)

Our first argument put us on a slippery slope moving swiftly towards desperation! Within the first nine months of our marriage, Carol and I were both convinced that we not only married the wrong person, but we were condemned to a loveless marriage as well. First of all, we were very young when we married, and we did not know the first thing about marriage. So, this alone caused us to have lots of ups and downs. We knew we loved each other. We just did not have the understanding about how to communicate well.

However, throughout the years we did learn how to converse with each other and how not to fight so much. As we kept God before our marriage, our union became stronger and stronger.

One very noticeable side effect of our difficulties was poor communication. She would ask, "Where have you been?" I would respond, "Out and about". She would always have to find me and it was not always good places to be found. She would say, "Again, tonight? This has to stop, Victor!" She would say, "What time are you coming home?" But then, I would hear, "You better get here and help me with the kids because you are never here!"

We could not express anything the way we really wanted to. We resorted to hurting each other with our words. We did not build each other up. We constantly tore each other down and caused deep emotional pain. Quite honestly, we had endured so much hurt and hurting each other that we could not see any hope of ever communicating well. Our despair was overwhelming.

We began learning about intentional communication in counseling. I remember thinking, "That is the stupidest thing I've ever heard. This stuff is so simple. I can't believe I'm paying this guy for this."

But once I got off of my high horse, I realized something very simple yet profound. If communication was really that simple, everyone would be doing it, and all of our communication would glorify God and reflect His image (1 Peter 4:11; Ephesians 4:29). Glorifying God did not represent my communication and it may not represent yours either. In fact, many of us struggle to communicate well even with those we love the most: our siblings, our parents, our children, and our spouse. The road I took to learn about communication was a tough one. Here are a couple of things that helped transform our marriage and change my heart:

The Principle of First Response

You may feel it's okay to strike at someone verbally because, "He is picking a fight with me." You may be correct, but that person does not have the power to decide whether a fight actually occurs. That power rests with the responder. As Proverbs 15:1 says, "A gentle answer turns away wrath, but a harsh word stirs up anger."

Jesus has a well-worn track record with the Principle of First Response. Recall the times that the Scribes and the Pharisees came to question Him. They were the initiators in nearly all of their communication.

    Their intention was to defraud Jesus and corner Him. In how many cases were they successful? None! They failed because the power to decide the direction of each conflict rested with Jesus, the responder (Luke 20:19-26). The implications of following Jesus' example were huge. My wife's sin did not give me free license to sin in return. And conversely, my sin did not give Carol free license either. By following the Principle of First Response, we were being called to take a poorly spoken comment and redirect it.

<u>The Principle of Physical Touch</u>

    This is a difficult principle to apply after an argument has begun. However, a perfect time is when you know you are about to sit down and have a discussion about something that might lead to tension. You know what those topics are in your marriage. Maybe it's a conversation about a specific child. Maybe it's your in-laws or your finances. For us, as you might imagine, it was when we sat down to talk about our communication issue. Those were tough conversations. During these times, we would sit down and pray together – and touch. Usually, we were at opposite ends of the couch with Carol's legs stretched out across mine while I held them.

The Principle of Physical Touch - It is difficult to sin against someone while you are tenderly touching them. (You may prefer holding hands or sitting close enough that you naturally touch). As we talked, we would inevitably notice something. When our conversation began to drift toward conflict, we stopped touching. We found what I am certain you will find: It is very difficult to fight with someone you are tenderly touching!

So, we had a choice at that point, to stop fighting so we could keep on touching or to stop touching so we could keep on fighting. We found that it takes lots of growth in this marriage and you will find the same for you too. Your relationship with your spouse may differ from ours, but this much is true: Your spouse should be the single most important person you have in your life.

Like it or not, communication is the tool that God has given us to knit our hearts and our minds together. Success is possible if we're willing to apply some intentional principles. We've all been called to God-honoring communication. Step forward in humility and faith and watch Him transform you.

LESSON 4

WHICH COMES FIRST ~ MARRIAGE OR MINISTRY?

"...But He That Is Married Careth For..."

(1 Corinthians 7:33-35)

But he that is married careth for the things that are of the world, how he may please his wife. There is a difference also between a wife and a virgin. The unmarried woman careth for the things of the Lord, that she may be holy both in body and in spirit: but she that is married careth for the things of the world, how she may please her husband. And this I speak for your own profit; not that I may cast a snare upon you, but for that which is comely, and that ye may attend upon the Lord without distraction.

(1Corinthians 7:33-35 KJV)

You will be surprised at how many people get this wrong!

For instance, a godly single woman has a privilege as she waits for her natural mate she can spend a lot of time with the Lord. She is pure in body and in spirit as she takes that time to become one and into intimacy with Him and Him alone.

For this is the will of God, your sanctification: that you abstain from sexual immorality: that each one of you know how to control his own body in holiness and honor, not in passion of lust like Gentiles who do not know God that no one transgress and wrong his brother in this matter, because the Lord is an avenger in all these things, as we told you beforehand and solemnly warned you. For God has not called us impurity, but in holiness...

(1 Thessalonians 4:3-7)

Many times, single women want to be married so soon. But if they only knew it is a time to now go at a greater demotion. A married woman has to take her time to be one with her husband taking care of his needs physically, sexually, and spiritually as well as the care of her children. Her family then God, it's called balance.

There were many times I had to put my family first. I sometimes worked 12/16 hours a day, got off work and still had to cook, clean, help my children with homework, pamper my Husband after everyone was in bed, then I would take that time to spend with the Lord.

As my husband worked along by helping as a team, taking turns to cook, clean, going to work to provide for the family, he too had to find that time to spend with the Lord.

1. So, which comes first, marriage or ministry?

_____
_____
_____
_____
_____

MARRIAGE MINISTRY WORKING TOGETHER WITH FAMILY

2. When ministry is put before marriage, how strong can a marriage be?

_____
_____
_____
_____
_____

3. Comments:

_____
_____
_____
_____
_____

LESSON 5

HEALTHY MARRIAGE

" Let thy fountain be blessed: and rejoice with the wife of thy youth."

(Proverbs 5:18)

Keep on with dating even AFTER the wedding. All those weeks and months of special date nights doesn't suddenly cease after the pastor pronounces you husband and wife. Experience taught us years ago to put date night into our plans before anything else goes into the schedule. There were lots of times when things seemed to get stressful, we simply would stop whatever we were doing and we would go on a date. It is so important; It does not matter whether you go out or stay in. For us; it often depended on our children (while they were still living at home), and finances also were a factor, for years.

If you're staying home, don't just do what you normally would do in the evening. Make it a special time with the best china for dinner, candles on the table, take a bubble bath together, have a good pillow fight, arm wrestle, and learn to give great massages, (dot, dot, dot, as they say in Mamma Mia).

When dating, date someone that is not pulling you out of the church; someone that is moving you forward into God. Being good is not going to get you into heaven, you must be born again. I'm not saying you are unequally yoked; yet, when my husband and I first got together neither one of us was saved.

While we were together, not yet married, I gave my life to the Lord. Victor did go to church; however, he was that one who felt as long as he went to church on Sunday that was all he needed. On the other hand, I came up in the "holiness" church, and I was determined that I was going to pull him into "holiness" with me. I believed that as I continued to stay saved and live that life in front of him, one day it would draw him to the Lord in a greater level. The word of God says, "What does light and darkness have in common?"(2 Corinthians 6:14).

We don't encourage you to get someone from the world, but let God give you your mate. You must have the gift of the spirit operating in your life with discernment so you can have an ear to hear. Don't be pulled by the lies of the devil. Dating the wrong way will get you the wrong mate.

1. Why is it so important to date?

_____
_____
_____
_____
_____

2. Why should we have the discernment of the Spirit? (1 Corinthians 12:7)

_____
_____
_____
_____
_____

3. If you date the wrong way what can happen? (2 Corinthians 6:14-18)

_____
_____
_____
_____
_____

4. Comments:

_____
_____
_____
_____
_____

LESSON 6

PRAYER: PRAY TIGHTER

"Father bless and strengthen are marriage in the midst of the pressure and problems of our lives,"

(2Corinthians 12:9)

The Principle of Prayer: Success is more likely when we invite God to be an active participant and guide. This principle is not complicated, but it requires our close attention. We've become so accustomed to hearing about prayer that its importance often passes us by. No matter what principle you might be using at the time or what subject you might be talking about, nothing is beyond prayer. I have tended to overestimate my own ability to communicate well and righteously. That was evidenced in our first year of marriage.

We will eventually and inevitably sin in our converse with each other when it begins to drift away from God's intended purpose for it; we have a choice: Will we be puffed up with pride or will we have the humility to stop right where we are and ask God to help redeem our conversation? The reason why many fail in battle is because they wait until the hour of battle. The reason why others succeed is because they have gained their victory on their knees long before the battle came.

Anticipate your battles; fight them on your knees before temptation comes, and you will always have victory. One of the greatest difficulties that couples face with this principle is awkwardness. They are not used to praying together. So, as they begin to like each other less in the midst of unconstructive communication, the thought of praying together is not very appealing.

We learned an easy fix to this – start praying together. Begin with 30 seconds of prayer as you go to bed each night, pray. The transformation never ends. As a result of God's grace intersecting with these principles, prayer and communication is now among the greatest strengths of our marriage. It's not that we don't still mess-up, we do.

Thankfully, God continues to work on us. He'll continue to work on you, too.

Prayers: Father I plead that we would speak the truth in Love to each other honestly and openly sharing our feeling with each other. (Ephesians 4:15, 25)

LESSON 7

SEXUAL INTIMACY

Drink waters out of thine own cistern, and running waters out of thine own well. Let thy fountains be dispersed abroad, and rivers of waters in the streets. Let them be only thine own, and not strangers' with thee. Let thy fountain be blessed: and rejoice with the wife of thy youth. Let her be as the loving hind and pleasant roe; let her breasts satisfy thee at all times; and be thou ravished always with her love.

(Proverbs 5:15-19)

There is a clear message in these verses that sex within marriage is a happy, fun, dynamic interaction that builds intimacy and authentic love.

Anticipation is very powerful: Talking about it, leaving little notes, kissing often, sending an anticipatory text message, having coded hints even when in front of the children or other people that they will never know the clue of what's going on but you two will; it is also a great stress reliever.

Within the Old Testament, no book captures God's feelings about His design for sex in marriage better than the Song of Solomon (also referred to as Song of Songs, and Canticles). We have the romantic interchange between a young husband and his wife. A detailed study reveals:

1. **God created the institution of marriage, and designed sex to be the ultimate intimacy-creator. From this book we can draw the following observations:**

- Romance is referred to as intoxicating, like wine, we are encouraged to make ourselves drunk with love!

- Song of Solomon contains detailed descriptions of sexual fullness between a young husband and wife. Bible scholars would agree that there are direct references to sex, and that sexuality is expressed without shame, is honorable, and a significant part of any marriage!

2. **The view that sex is "bad" or should not be spoken about is certainly not supported from the Bible!**

3. **The Minor Prophets Section ~ Scriptures on Marriage and Sex**

- Hosea ~ here we have the story of a marriage gone bad fast. It is a rather depressing story of one of God's prophets (Hosea) who is instructed to marry a prostitute (named Gomer)!

- This young lady marries Hosea, but eventually returns to her prostitution.

- We find out that the story is also a metaphor of the relationship between God and His people, Israel, in the Old Testament.

- Though God loved them, they returned to their sin, and left Him just as Gomer left Hosea.

- Through this sad tale we glean one exciting idea: marriage is a picture of God and His love for His people!

4. The Law Section ~ Scriptures on Marriage and Sex

- In the Old Testament, the Law of God was revealed to the Jewish people, with prohibitions on certain sexual activity that was present within other cultures:

- **Adultery**: sex outside of marriage (Leviticus 20:10; Deuteronomy 22:22; Hebrews 13:4)

- **Incest:** sex with a close relative (Leviticus 18)

- **Homosexuality:** in both the Old Testament God strongly condemns sexual relations with a person of the same gender (Leviticus 18:22; Leviticus 20:13), and in the New Testament (Romans 1:24-28)

- **Rape:** (Deuteronomy 22:23-29)

- **Fornication:** consensual sex with one other than your mate (Exodus 22:16,17)

- **Prostitution:** God stated He hates it (Deuteronomy 23:17,18)

- **Bestiality:** a perversion detested by God (Leviticus 20:15, 1)

1. Read the story and give your revelation/ understanding on sexual intimacy? (answers with scripture)

_____
_____
_____
_____
_____

2. Why is there a must for intimacy in your marriage? (answers with scripture)

_____
_____
_____
_____
_____

3. Comments:
___
___
___
___
___

LESSON 8

THE VOWS

(Number 30:2-8)

What are the vows for? Why would it say "…for better or for worse; for richer, for poorer; in sickness and in health …", if it didn't mean just that? There will come a time when the money might run low, or one of you may become ill, or maybe the both of you may become ill, and there's sometimes one may make more money than the other. Nevertheless, we should never put the other down to break this God-given covenant between each other.

This is a promise when once made we are to keep. The Bible says, "If a man or a woman vow a vow unto the Lord, or swear an oath to bind his soul with a bond he shall do according to all that proceeded out of his mouth" (Number 30: 2-8). I remember a time when my husband was injured on his job. The injury caused him to come off work for a long time. I had to work to keep the bills paid up. I never once complained about him being sick and how I had the responsibility to pay the bills.

I just did as the vow said, "...for poorer, in sickness ..." We stayed together in love, some of those times were hard, but the good Lord made a way. There was a time that I became sick and had to come off work, and my husband did the same for me, and we are still together. We kept the promise.

Vows defined as: Voluntary promises which, when once made, were to be kept if the thing vowed was right. They were made under a great variety of circumstances (Gen. 28: 18-22; Lev. 7:16; Num. 30:2-13; Deut. 23:18; Judg. 11:30, 39; 1 Sam. 1:11; Jonah 1:16; Acts 18:18; 21:23).[1]

1. **Question & Answers: What does the vows stand for? (In a plain sentence with scripture)**

_____

_____

_____

_____

_____

2. Prior to this session, what was your understanding about "the vows"?

_____

_____

_____

_____

_____

3. Comments:

_____

_____

_____

_____

_____

LESSON 9

UNEQUALLY YOKED

Do not be Unequally Yoked together

*(*2 Corinthians 6:14)

This unequally yoked scripture is one of those Bible verses that, if we will understand its principle, will save us a lot of heartache and in all honesty, unsatisfactory marriages.

What Is The Definition Of The Unequally Yoked Bible Verse?

When you yoke something together, it means to tie them together like oxen in a harness pulling a wagon or team horses pulling a stagecoach. It means you are fitting them together to work as a team. So with this definition of unequally yoked, let's look at the Bible verse that uses this metaphor in regards to marriage.

Do not be unequally yoked together with unbelievers. For what fellowship has righteousness with lawlessness? And what communion has light in darkness?

2 Corinthians 6:14 - (NKJV)

The Temple of the Living God Don't team up with those who are unbelievers. How can righteousness be a partner with darkness? How can light live with darkness?

2 Corinthians 6:14 - (NLT)

I gave you this scripture in two different translations. I want you to fully understand what it is saying. Most people just repeat the first part of the verse like it was a commandment; he was trying to get the people to understand how important is to be equally yoked with the Lord Jesus Christ. He was trying to show that we have to look at marriage from a totally different light than just whether or not we have attached emotional reactions to them. He wants us to step back and see weather or not they fit!

This Principle is to be equally yoked, not to avoid being unequally yoked.

Paul is making a case here in this Bible verse to make sure you are equally yoked with God, and he used an extreme example of a believer marrying an unbeliever. However, this principle goes way deeper then whether or not someone has accepted Jesus as their Lord and Savior or not. It goes into a key ingredient of a healthy relationship. Fellowship (being a partner) and Communion (living intimately) and this stands for all believers not to have any part in darkness.

This principle can be applied to just more than marriage. You can apply this principle to see if your relationships are unequally yoked, or if your business partnerships are unequally yoked, and most especially if you are practicing unequally yoked dating. God wants the best for you, so have faith in that, and believe that God loves you enough to give you His best by giving you a true partner and person you can live with intimately.

LESSON 10

UNDERSTANDING HOW TO CHOOSE YOUR MATE

"Whoso findeth a wife findeth a good thing, and obtaineth favour of the Lord."

(Proverbs 18:22)

1. Never choose a man, any man, over your children.

- When I say 'any man', this does not mean a God-fearing man, but this person has a background of abuse, molestation, etc. This area in his life has not been dealt with. In other words, just know when choosing your mate the important thing is for him to have salvation on top of the discerning, of the spirit. The Word of God says, "A man that finds a wife, finds a good thing". Now, am I contradicting the Word of God by saying a "woman"?

- No, because a woman can choose her mate by the Spirit of God. That's why it's so important to be in a place with God to hear what's best for your family and marriage.

2. To allow a man, including a husband to hurt your child is the height of selfishness, self-centeredness, and weakness.

3. The reason I say this is that, in time past, I have seen people allow men over their children saved and unsaved that just were not good for them or the children in which we believe was not the will of God. This sometimes can lead to abuse and molestation. Not only can it hurt the children but it also destroys the whole family. So we believe God should be the center of all marriages as well as the family.

4. No matter what he provides, no matter how much you love him, no matter how long you have been married, don't bring an unworthy man into your children's lives or your family. And when we say 'unworthy' we don't mean in a way that God sees him, but in a way that he allows his life to be controlled by Satan and he can only see from a dark-side view.

5. The right to meet your children needs is an earned right. To me, the child needs are the covering from a biblical truth standard. It says, "To train up a child in the way he should go and when he grows old, he will not depart from it." I believe that we have a covenant right over our child until they are of a particular age, so until is to, cover for every in pray but it will come a time they will need to make a choice of their own.

6. Your job is to protect the life that you gave them with the wisdom from God.

7. Never let your children see a man hurt you. You are writing the story of their childhood, be careful what memories you allow to be written in their hearts and minds. This story could cost them a lifetime.

8. Your children may except being abused, or receive things in their hearts or minds to make them feel unworthy, and begin to feel this is a normal way of life, and may have a hard time being able to build healthy relationships.

9. The word of God said, "but if ye shall at all turn from following me, ye or your children, and will not keep my commandments and my statutes which I have set before you, but go and serve other gods, and worship them:" (1King 9:6)

10. "Ah sinful nation, a people laden with iniquity, a seed of evil-doers, children that deal corruptly! they have forsaken Jehovah, they have despised the Holy One of Israel, they are estranged and gone backward." (Isaiah 1:4 ASV)

11. "A seed the children of wicked parents whose guilt they follow corrupter themselves or others by their counsel and example backward instead of proceeding forward and growing in Grace."[2]

MARRIAGE MINISTRY WORKING TOGETHER WITH FAMILY

QUESTIONS & ANSWERS

1. Why is it so important to understand how to choose your mate? (In a plain sentence with scripture)

___

2. Why should you not choose a mate over children?

___

3. Why is it your job to protect your children?

_____
_____
_____
_____
_____

4. Comments:

_____
_____
_____
_____
_____

CONCLUSION

CAROL'S OUTLOOK: HISTORY

My husband and I have been married for 29 years. We still treat each other like high school sweethearts. Even though there was someone before him, my husband still fits that place in my heart as my first love; no one can ever take the place of him. I returned to Albion, Michigan from Houston, Texas in 1985, with two small children and connected with 'my' Victor. We were married four years later in 1989, and we have been in love ever since. Also, I gave my life to the Lord a month before we were married.

We have a total of four children, two together and two from my prior union. My husband never likes me to explain it like that because he has helped take care of them just like his own and he loves them the same. My husband is a provider and a very hard worker who loves to take care of his family. All of our children are grown up at this point.

VICTOR'S OUTLOOK: CAROL

She's my sweetheart. She is like a mother, a father, a sister and a brother. No one can ever take her place. She stood in the gap for me when I was out in the world doing the wrong thing. I have always promised her that I was going to do everything I could to make her and the family happy. I have done that, and I am still doing it with the help of God Almighty. Carol is a very good mother who always takes the time to put good and God in our children. I truly thank God for her. Sometimes people fail to see all the 'behind the scene' things my wife does.

She is a very strong woman of God, a faithful wife, and mother to our kids and me. I love her so very much. We grew up together, and we made mistakes together. Once we had a big falling-out and she just knew this was it! My response to her was, "I told God I was going to stay married to you and I'm not going to let you make a liar out of me." Well, that statement shut her right up! Still, we take all our experiences to make and mold us into the couple we are today. We always knew that a marriage relationship ministry was there; but we did not know what it looked like, how we would accomplish it, or even when it would start.

ABOUT THE AUTHOR

Pastor Carol Brown is a woman of vision and virtue. She has lived in Albion, Michigan most of her life. She got saved at the age of twenty-one when she gave her heart to Jesus Christ. For over 28 years, she has been in church serving the Lord faithfully. She is also a gifted Prophetess and operates in deliverance ministry. She is known as a prophetic intercessor. She has received training from many anointed ministers. She was ordained by Apostle Jean Smith. In 2010, Pastor Carol received a diploma when she graduated from the "First Foundational Steps in God" class.

God woke Pastor Carol out of her sleep when He called her to ministry. He spoke to her and said, "I want you to help the unlearned, poor and needy!" A month later, God spoke to her again but this time in a dream. He gave her the name of her current church. This is how "Build Them On The Rock Ministries" was born.

Carol is married to Victor Brown. They have five children and nine grandchildren who they love very much. Carol and her husband are pastor & co- pastor of "Build Them On the Rock Training Center Ministries".

They along with their son, were the first three members. Shortly thereafter, their daughter and granddaughter joined. The ministry continues to grow. Souls are being saved and lives are being changed through the ministry.

REFERENCES

1. Vow. (n.d.). Easton Bible Dictionary. Retrieved from http://eastonsbibledictionary.org/3777-Vows.php

2. Wesley, J. (n.d.). Chapter 1 Isaiah Wesley Explanation Notes. Retrieved from www.biblestudytools.com/commentaries/wesley-explanatory-notes/isaiah/isaiah-1.html

INDEX

A

Adultery, 32
Albion, 47, 49
Anticipation, 30

B

balance, 20
battle, 27
Bestiality, 33

C

children, 7, 11–12, 15, 20, 22, 30, 41–49
church, 23, 49
cleave, 8
commandments, 39, 44
communion, 39–40
conflict, 16–17
conversation, 16–17, 27
counseling, 14

D

darkness, 23, 39–40

desperation, 13
discernment, 24
distraction, 18
Divided, 7
dreams, 49

E

emotional pain, 14

F

faith, 17, 40
families, 20, 42, 47–48
fellowship, 39–40
Fornication, 32

G

gift, 24
grace, 10, 44

H

hearts, 15, 17, 43, 47, 49
holiness, 19, 23
Holy Spirit, 10
humility, 17, 27
hurt, 14, 42–43
hurting, 14

I

Incest, 32
intimacy, 19, 29, 33
intimidation, 8
intoxicating, 30

L

Lord, 8–9, 18–20, 23, 35–36, 40–41, 47, 49

M

marriage, 10, 13–18, 20–21, 26–27, 29–33, 38–40, 42
marriage ministry, 9
metaphor, 31, 38
midst, 26–27
ministry, 7, 9–10, 18, 20–21, 49–50
mother, 8, 48

P

parents, 15
partner, 11, 39–40
person, 13, 15, 17, 32, 40–41
power, 15–16
Praise, 11
prayer, 8, 10, 26–28
praying, 27
principle, 16, 26–27, 38, 40
promise, 8, 35–36

R

Rape, 32

rejoice, 22, 29
responder, 15–16
responsibility, 35
revelation, 33
righteousness, 39
Rock Ministries, 49

S

sanctification, 19
self-centeredness, 42
selfishness, 42
sexual immorality, 19
sexual relations, 32
sickness, 35–36
stress reliever, 30

T

transformation, 27
truth, 28

U

unbelievers, 39–40
unified-front, 7
union, 14

V

victory, 27
vows, 35–36, 51

W

weaknesses, 8, 42

www.ingramcontent.com/pod-product-compliance
Lightning Source LLC
Chambersburg PA
CBHW041959080526
44588CB00021B/2802